Aeolian Harp
volume 1

Edited by Ralph Hamilton & Ami Kaye

Guest Editor: Ralph Hamilton
Series Editor: Ami Kaye
Project Manager: Royce Ellen Hamel
Layout, Book & Cover Design: Steven M. Asmussen
Copyediting: Linda Kim
Cover Artist: Tracy McQueen

Fonts "National Oldstyle", "Persnickety", and "Metro Thin" designed by Andrew Leman, courtesy of The H. P. Lovecraft Historical Society, www.cthulhulives.org"

Aeolian Harp Series: Anthology of Poetry Folios
Volume 1
Copyright © 2016 Glass Lyre Press, LLC
Paperback ISBN: 978-1-941783-16-0

All rights reserved: except for the purpose of quoting brief passages for review, no part of this book may be reproduced or transmitted in any form or by any means, electronic or mechanical, including photocopying, recording, or by any information storage and retrieval system, without permission in writing from the publisher.

Glass Lyre Press, LLC
P.O. Box 2693
Glenview, IL 60026

www.GlassLyrePress.com

Preface

Ami Kaye, Series Editor

The wind flows between the strings of an Aeolian harp and emerges as music in much the same way poetry magically alters our response to language. We enter the realm of beauty, pain, fear, and wonder. The rhythms of poetry echo our iambic heartbeats, liberating images and metaphors, words that spark and ignite our imaginations. While most anthologies are arranged thematically with insights on particular topics, to search for the elusive, to name what cannot be named, to express what is difficult to say but universally true, the Aeolian Harp Series offers a unique format in which ten poets are spotlighted in a more intimate setting with individual sections devoted to their folios—a collection of some of their best, representative work.

The quality of an anthology depends heavily on the hand that curates the work, and we count ourselves fortunate to have the talents of Ralph Hamilton for this debut volume. Ralph is the editor-in-chief of the highly regarded RHINO Poetry. In addition to his top-notch editing skills, Ralph is also a poet of exceptional talent. His selections and input for this issue have been nothing short of remarkable, and we are indebted to him for his patience and diligence.

Most of all, we extend our gratitude to all the submitting poets for this project, especially our authors. The ten poets in this volume are highly accomplished, selected for their unique and diverse voices. Their folios provide a feast of poetry, a variety of styles and treatments, a way to experience each single poem as it opens our eyes and senses, winding its way to our hearts.

Foreword

Ralph Hamilton, Guest Editor

You must believe: a poem is a holy thing—a good poem, that is.
—Theodore Roethke

Perhaps some poets write out of soul-sick cynicism or smarty-pants swagger. But not the poems that follow here. This anthology comes from somewhere else entirely: from a need to witness to what has been seen and deeply felt, from what has been experienced and survived, from what has profoundly transformed each poet's way of being-in-the-world, if only for a moment.

For these poets something vital, something lived, something desperate is at stake in their work. In these psalms, incantations, fables, psychic bloodlines, taxonomies of light, homilies, epiphanies, epistles, elegies, odes, revenants and raptures, what is at stake is everything.

These poems demonstrate again and again that only poetry—with its breath-born rhythms and sonic landscapes, its vast palettes, potent images and startling leaps, its formal constraints and reckless possibilities—is capable of evoking the dense, allusive, and intricate contradictions of being alive. And only poetry can approach the reality of mystery, the legitimacy of wonder, and the possibility of meaning, without falling into either sophistry or nihilism.

For instance, Gail Goepfert's reveries summon readers' senses to the ecstasy of attention, showing how noticing some insignificant thing—opening one's mind and body to its unlikely facticity, its distinctive features, how it teases the light or plays with the wind—can rescue a person from dullness, or pain, or emptiness:

> *Like silk stockings*
> *on a clothesline,*
> *they come to me,*
> *the leaves of red-oak*
> *hydrangea, nodding*

> *diaphanous in the lap*
> *of afternoon.*

With a similar acuity, Nicole Rollender brings to life a piece of family history, with vivid and earthy precision:

> *I've imagined my great-grandmother in love,*
> *her hands deep in a pig's meat she rolled*
> *into sausages. Blood's aldehydic stench. Large clocks*
> *laughing all over the house. Massive dark beds. Her long dress*
> *licking the top of her foot.*

Terry Savoie, meanwhile, depicts the effulgence and flurries of seasonal change in an ordinary farmyard:

> *Huckleberries blue beneath*
>
> *September suns; pullets*
> *feather out on garden wastes & ants*
> *in cantaloupes as cockerels*
>
> *crow & crow*
> *like rasps drawn backwards*
> *across the ends of copper tubing.*

Like long-lost diary entries or letters, Susan Tepper's linked prose poems summon a bygone time and place, yet remain redolent with a familiar loss and yearning:

> *The child is buried near the hill where bluebells grow. It was smaller*
> *than my palm. The day hung still with yellow light.*

And Peggy Dobreer's description of wings in motion captures the ineffable connection among things adored:

> *…A motion*
> *without thought is*
> *pure mother, perfect*

> *flight, request answered.*
>
> *Golden, glimmering like*
> *a whisper, faint but sure,*
> *on the ear of the beloved.*

Embedded in a history of people and place, Joseph Fasano addresses the disordering power of revelation that is both refuge and risk:

> *I would tell you of the wide hours of surrender,*
>
> *when the river stripped the cove's stones*
> *from the margin and the blackbirds built*
> *their strict songs in the high*
>
> *pines, when the great nest swayed the lattice*
> *of the branches, the moon's brute music*
> *touching them with fire.*

Margo Berdeshevsky's poem about a woman confronting her mortality speculates on the modes of her departure, but concludes with an austere generosity:

> *Too young to be skeletal, skin taken wing.*
> *Bone no longer needed. Dove.*
> *Fire-eyed. Distant. Opal.*
>
> *The root does not care*
> *where her water comes from.*
> *Here is another thirsty body.*
> *Broken into morning.*

Exploring the painter Utrillo, Bill Yarrow reveals the artist's lonely consciousness and stern singular vision:

> *Overhead, mawkish gulls begin to weep daylight into the marsh.*
> *The gutters blush as men in bloody aprons take their business to their*

> walls. Priests in red robes bend their tonsures toward eternity, or so it seems to him, supine, head wedged against the bookcase, mouth agape, dreaming of dangers, his feet perpendicular to the floor.

While Susan Cohen reveals the uncanny link between beauty and destruction in her home state:

> *This light began in lamentation,*
> *but I don't want to think*
> *about the unmaking, the burning*
> *hopes and homes a hundred miles*
> *from here. This light is strangely*
> *sewn with honey as if thimbled*
> *from the flight of bees.*

Again and again these poets ask us to reconsider the normal, to rediscover the numinous power in the most regular habits and objects; thus even sleep, in its capacity to shift the world upon waking, does not escape Rustin Larson's pen:

> *You won't recognize the sun*
> *When you wake, or how the trees have become*
> *A different room, or how their scent is on you*
>
> *Something like a stain, a handprint, a ghost,*
> *A goddess of rivers, a song broken.*

Each of these poets in her or his own way has staked a claim on the world. A claim on life. Although steeped in singular histories and the particulars of different places, these poems suggest the redemptive and generative power of language itself. In each of them the world—its lived reality, its pain, its wonder, its mystery—is reborn. That is, I believe, the radical meaning behind Roethke's use of the word "holy" in the epigraph with which this introduction began:

> *You must believe: a poem is a holy thing—a good poem, that is.*

Read on, and see for yourself.

...this harp which I wake now for thee
   Was a siren of old who sung under the sea.

— Thomas Moore, *The Origin of the Harp*

Folios

Gail Goepfert	13
Nicole Rollender	23
Terry Savoie	33
Susan Tepper	43
Peggy Dobreer	51
Joseph Fasano	59
Margo Berdeshevsky	67
Bill Yarrow	79
Susan Cohen	87
Rustin Larson	93

Gail Goepfert

As a photographer, I marvel at my inability to recreate an image. Each click of the shutter captures a single moment—the meeting of light, subject, and angle—nearly impossible to duplicate. So too with poetry. Poems are so often "of the moment." I love poetry's restless variety, how it reflects the unpredictability of things. And yet, the uncertainties of change can result in a more cautious voice, tempered by my attention to particulars, those fine details that become part of balancing content, style, and language. As I draft, my words evolve in an organic fashion on the page—perhaps not surprising given my kinship with so much that is visual. I enjoy experimenting with an eye toward mirroring the persistent and fleeting, the robust and the fragile. There are endless influences to admire. Yesterday, Louise Gluck may have been my guru, but tomorrow it may be Ross Gay or Ruth Stone or Wendell Berry

In many things, I am a witness. Visual particulars pull me away, things others might not notice—a droplet clinging to a red berry or light through veined leaves. A few years back on a trip to Williamsburg, Virginia, I shopped at a mini-mall filled with room after room of touristy goods. My focus came back to a storefront display of oversized paper umbrellas not unlike the miniatures in tropical drinks. They filled the giant windows, and the light poured through. I circled back again and again taking shot after shot of these vibrant umbrellas not even for sale. Serendipity. In framing the photos, I cropped out the surrounding kitsch, capturing only the swirl and rhythm of colored paper itself. Sometime later, one of these photographs became a cover for a Japanese-themed poetry issue of *Rattle*. I love that I have two artistic passions in which the chance intersections of image and word can materialize. Image, color, and light texture the language of my writing. I am exquisitely drawn to specifics, to the limitations and promise of language and craft to express myself—my way to decipher what it means to be alive.

Drinking It In

It is morning. I sit on the sunporch
in a spill of wintered geraniums.

Hail-pearls stamp hard-edged brick and glass.
Punctuate all sound.

Early spring sidles in. A ladle of ocean,
a scull across the salt-lipped sea.

Witness! The alchemy of eye to eye, rib to rib, thigh to mine.

Body's balm. Salty. Touch and shudder.
Shudder and touch.

I drink from the lip of the carafe. Quenched.

Knee in knee, a finger-trace of scar. Cheek rests
on an arm-curl of damp.

The pear juice puddles. Gone its thin rind
and honeyed flesh.

And there's champagne and shine and green
and wings to elevate.

I name each drop of rain, each seep of pear.

Dead Reckoning

Sometimes I need to take my own hand,
cast off from shore, concede
      on the cusp of a new moon
that I'm not lost.

For years, I've lived in layers
      plummeting into waters
unwarmed by light
      in uncharted depths
      clutching
at what swims past.

I'll learn to revere white space—
      open to infinite edges, pooling
on a page of warm light.
Let my wandering eye rest.
      I will know when I am home.

All of a summer afternoon,
      I'll stand
with my fisher grandfather
      spooling worms on hooks—
no need to untangle twisted threads.
      My faith
in a red-and-white bobber
      on the lake's swelling skin.

In the Glass of My Eye

I.

Floating threads
read
like stenciled shreds
of hieroglyphic
newsprint.

Speckled flies fly
before me
by day, by night,
sparklers
dart on the rim.

It is coming back to me.
Clearer vision.
Vitreous detachment—
another of body's ripening
imperfections.

II.

She's there.
On the lip
of my mind's eye.

My grandmother
skinning peaches,
plump globes of juicy

flesh in season,

crisscrossing
lard-dough
for the lattice-top pie,
blind-eyed
to her hunched spine,
her clock's tick-tock.

Light dims in a blink.

III.

How is it possible
that I taste with my eyes?

Like silk stockings
on a clothesline,
they come to me,
the leaves of red-oak
hydrangea, nodding

diaphanous in the lap
of afternoon.

Veins in crackled
ambered glass.

It's hard to brood.

I gather light
coming and going.

Longing for the Wind to Quiver Again
—after Geri Doran

Above, stars make
a slow-hipped pivot.
Branches thicken night—
and the litter of dropped pods
like constellations
map the weatherings
of the soul.

No solace in a stalled wind—
an elegy
in search of ease.

An updraft commences
in the pale morning air—
comfort in the hush hush.

The bicycle bell's jingle
       breaks through,
clear and clean as picked bone
like the luminous cells in me.

Can I settle into the stretch of skin
I was given at birth?
I refuse to hush
the beebox inside me.

Reading the Bookshelf Sideways

Here
in the gray limbo of perhaps
where I live—
nineteen hats, ten teacups, an empty birdcage
& the art of longing.
Longing for the ocean at the end of the lane,
for a suitcase of seaweed, crocus
in the snow, green winter,
longing for the lessons
of the good body.

I embrace the places that scare me—
nightdances from the belly,
conversations with myself, sailing
alone around the room.
A night without armor.
I wait for the hollering sun—
forego deathwatch
before numbering the bones.

The world doesn't end.
Many winters, springing,
delights and shadows, the all of it.
A strike sparks
a fire in my hands.

Authors of books in the order their titles appear: Wislawa Szymborska, Maxine Kumin, Kate Hutchinson, Cooper Eden, Neil Gaiman, Janet S. Wong, Joan Walsh Anglund, Elise Maclay, Joanne Diaz, Anne Becker, James Scofield, Virginia Bell, Nelson Mandela, Billy Collins, Jewel, Nancy Wood, Robb White, Ann Rinaldi, Charles Simic, Nancy Wood, Marie Ponsot, Ted Kooser, Jeanette Haien Sharon Olds, Gary Soto.

Get Up, Said the World

—after Louise Glück's "October"

I.

Is it near-winter again, is it cold again,
didn't the snow just pool
among the winter pansies, the bed-ivy,

didn't the pavement
dampen with melt, melt slosh
on suede boots,

didn't ice daggers just
slither down the shingles

piercing the ear, the sallow earth
in their plummet?
I remember how russet

turned to olive to meadow green,
moss threading the bricks
like damask.

Didn't I just hear the jay?

No matter the apricot
on the rose, the banjo tuned
when the cicadas come.

I am silenced. Empty.

By the gravity of winters
past, the cruelty of hollows
in the days that shamble by

savagely the same.

Foolish. I look for reclamation
in rusty soup kettles,
joints that creak.

The breadknife's in the marrow.

There's no retreat,
from the caustic lime
tapped into that fissure.

II.

Only red berries
fleck the crabapple bough—leafskins
like snake jackets upon the ground.

Tell me I'm wrong.
Tell me the drained rain barrel
bubbles over
come spring.

I swallow hard in the dark.

Tell me numbed and frozen flesh
rouses with touch.

My feet root in the dank.

I listen for what I know.

Listen for a ping, a quiver
beneath my ribs.

III.

It is true that some things
are beyond my ken.
I swing vine-like
between wise and withered.

It's true. In spring, fiddleheads
push through the earth.

Curlicues of green
uncoil in the sun.

But it is gray that taps me dry.

Wanting, I wrench
brilliance from sunlight.

IV.

Get up, said the world.

I try to make a sonnet
out of charcoal.

Nicole Rollender

photo: Rick Urbanowski Photography

In my writing, I marry the melancholic and the celebratory, the disordered with the ordered, the grotesque and the gorgeous. My poems aren't for everyone: they're self-confrontational and not meant to be comfortable, but I work to create a kind of beauty from what most disturbs us, like poems about the dead – and what haunts us. And also for those seeking what the divine is / means / how it speaks and manifests.

The narrator in my poems is many: women who talk to the dead, women who mourn dead mothers and grandmothers, women suicides, women who've been raped / escaped rape, women who cradle premature babies, women who suffer depression, women who prepare the bodies of the dead, women who exist between their children's bodily needs and saints' incorruptible bodies. These women also live inside themselves, contending with the wolves within. The dead, the living, and the divine inhabit my poems – they're looking for kinship, remembrance, for some kind of communion. These poems are about the struggle of living in a body, being a parent, trying to find the balance between what our lives on earth mean / what it means to come to terms with dying.

The idea of having a female lineage that goes back and forward is part of the way of having both a history to root oneself in and a way to live, perhaps forever, on both earth and in the afterlife, is loud in my poems. The dead grandmother, for example, often haunts my poems, seemingly as an archetype of this dead / but still living source of history, wisdom, comfort and also mischief. But also children. In my poems, the body evolves into a conduit, for the dead who enter and exit, and also for babies, who originate in the womb and then exit.

Finally, my poems evolve into artifact: They're my attempt to root in a particular moment in time or space, to remember – so that as our time on earth passes, we have a tangible space created in words that we can return to, to savor, to satisfy our nostalgia.

Psalm to be Read While my Daughter Looks at Her Ribs

Once I was a girl at the altar: dear communicant, kneel here: there was no saint under my veil: the painted female martyrs never smiled, but looked up into the nave: searching for the sun prismed through glass: the wounds on their backs tell a story: the stigmata's scabs painted in a silent field: a drowned saint looks up at terns crying above a sea: O, this field that's no more: to give up this earth is to sacrifice my body: my tiny-boned daughter traces her ribs: they're a boat's exposed scaffolding: she knows her body is made well: she doesn't know someday her body will fall apart and sleep under the flowers she also loves: this boat is at the bottom of the ocean: the first time she saw her bones illumined, the reflection of skin in the tilted mirror: it was love: holding up her hands as if doves would land there: the girl I was learned about submission: a tinge of teeth along pelvis: daughter, one day you may be asked to wear divinity in a field: orchid petals, a shawl: and so another world appears: these doves rising out of your throat are silent: yet they're louder than everything you love.

THE RETURN

for Florentine Bia

I've imagined my great-grandmother in love,
her hands deep in a pig's meat she was rolling

into sausages. Blood's aldehydic stench. Large clocks
laughing all over the house. Massive dark beds. Her long dress

licking the top of her foot. She remembered the geese
her mother strangled, the sound a whine just before

the final breath, the first time they made love. I didn't exist.
I wonder if she felt her own death, her hands limp

on the bed after, the wind pulled out of her,
if when she finally spoke, *look at the starlight,*

look, her voice meeting that light would carry forward
to this day, when I say aloud, *Florentine, Florentine,*

we are both alive in this poem, my hands deep in tomato hearts,
the man I've chosen to love somewhere in the garden,

his words still vibrating: What you do is wake
the dead. You don't let them sleep.

Bone of My Bone

I am my own land, unmanageable. There's a cross
    road where my hands and lips intersect

with an illumined city's windows open to blackbirds
    that promise to come through branches,

incising a woman's kitchen, the reliquaria of domesticity—
    white-draped ducks' broken necks rising

on counters. How do I measure the body's gardens
    from within its bone fences? A woman's skin

is one world. The birth canal is another—how you lived
    in a bell or in an oyster, rocking back and forth

in seaweed for a long time. Who hatches from it, shining
    through rain? In the old world, piss prophets mixed

a woman's lemon urine with wine to discern what
    was in the womb. A hand held out for a zinnia

if she empties, if a distant horse runs back
    to God, if a boat grows smaller, its cargo

of consecrated pears now rotting. My mother will curl
    into herself, as will I, as did my grandmother, joints

unloosening more than a century after her birth. I put
    the lines that grew on her skin into a bowl, muddy

my fingers in her waxiness and into her dead eye,
    unraveling her, seaming her skin, blanching her

bones back to such a shine, like a giant star's last open
    into brilliance. The unhurried light is dying, drunken

bees dropping into water, isn't it? My body is made
    from these flat-footed women—when I step

outside not knowing where I'm headed, one of them wakes
    from her dream of owls calling and hisses,

We created you from what we saved.

How to Talk to Your Dead Mother

At first, it's like old times, old bones: she puts
her hand on the inside of your lower arm's trusting
skin, a cat's belly turned up. She wants to know
about what she's missed—things that don't matter
as much to you—the swans on the lake, did their five
cygnets survive, or did a snapping turtle drag them
under the water, all except one? Her white dress
rustles, the tinkle of tiny finger bones in a pocket. She
remembers the hummingbird's ruby throat shimmering
still at the feeder. You tell her how your body failed,
the baby was born nine weeks early. Her hands make
the shape of wings. No, no, you say, he lived. *Can you
tell me again what it's like to be hungry? What does the body release
in sleep?* You say the hummingbird's too frantic to watch.
To keep the baby alive, you hold him over your heart,
skin on skin. Pray for mercy, for how the body hollows,
your mother intones, and that's how you remember
her—if you don't pray against everything, the roof
will fall in, the trees will pierce the windows, the quilts
go up in flames. You don't tell her how your whole life
has gone brittle, as if one shake will break every word
you try to substitute. She's your mother, now one who
returns trailing celestial afterbirth, a sort of innocence:
*Tell me what it feels like to put your foot in water. What does it
mean when you can't make any more milk for the child?* You
don't ask her to bless your house or the baby whose
bones rise against skin. Her hands have been in the earth.
Well, they are there now, folded in this quiet sacrament
of how what has been useful sleeps. You, the living
mother, shake salt from the table cloth, teach your
child to nest where it's warm, tell your dead to head
toward whatever window is full of light.

This is How to Feed Your Young

With your claws and beak, pull fish, pluck
what crawls. Feed the architecture of flight,

delicate tilt of radius and ulna, keeled breast
bone like a wheel of lightning, the lightness

of wing-truss spokes. Bone cleave and cleaving:
Bird and egg are one geography. The birds

observe the time of their migration. Some
abandon their eggs to follow far starlight

that ravens break open with their eyes.
Consider how nightjars trill the whole

brooding time: prayer beaks devouring
their own arrival. This feeding is a constant

thing, a shared consent. Hollow your throat
for its song, this watching, chick to beak,

this loop of hunger and to satisfy. There
are women who watch female birds rise,

look for auspices in the turning and cries.
According to scripture, the faithful birds

will assemble to eat the flesh of queens
and their horses. The ones who forsake

their young will have gizzards slashed out,
toes stuck fast in birdlime. Like the fallen

bird still turned toward the nest, you'll always
have pain near the wishbone, the distance

between your beaks unable to break or heal.

Reading Vallejo, On Having No Desires

Are you waiting for me in winter, next to an iced-
over pond, me in a red dress cutting open my belly,
how a days-dead doe exposes? Is that how you'd

like it? If you're waiting for me to turn in circles
until I fall over dizzy, well, any kind of desire
I've known doesn't arrive with a heart, and I won't

die with one. I pluck devotion's needles from
my palm, one claw at a time. I name you Sadness,
the one who slants long days, Desire's mirage of one

hand extended to repair the scars on my body's
geography: how we become that gravity. In the black
hole outside heaven, the workroom from where

God sends thirsts earthward to test the living,
or kill, I imagine He considers those who love
him, a few loose moths singeing around his flame.

The rest unravel him like a tongue, his cry passing
through the world's spine as a shudder that reminds
the trees even God can't escape himself. I've counted

wild branches for the dead to return as some other
thing, a bee's flight and then sting, a mea culpa
chanted in the chapel, even me shedding me,

loosening the body's carapace and saying I have
a new name: Winged baby of the ruins, Hands
holding eggs, Woman who wrings birds'

necks. Pray with me for the desire not to have
longings anymore, for me to cross out of my
borders. Your hand travels my body—this afternoon

lifts us out of ourselves, reminds me that no
matter how long or wildly we love, we still
need to lower our heads and drink again, again.

Terry Savoie

The pieces selected for this anthology represent poems written at various moments over several decades. It is difficult, if not impossible, to give a coherent aesthetic that covers such a lengthy period since aesthetic concerns change as one's body, environment, and needs evolve. Now, nearing seventy, my bent is toward the quiet poem with a spiritual center to it, something which certainly may not be fashionable. That said, there have been a few guiding influences over the years that deserve at least a passing recognition. I attended the Iowa Writers' Workshop's MFA program for a year although, since that time, I have written and worked in isolation.

Influences have come almost exclusively from my reading of a wide range of poets including Levine, Merwin, Niedecker, Ponsot, Milosz, Levertov, Justice, Stern, Berryman, and Williams, but already the list has grown far too long without a mention of hundreds of others in a library that my wife complains doesn't know when enough actually is enough. Simply said: I read, read, and reread. Moreover, allow me to include specific biographical facts that have influenced my aesthetic: service in mental hospitals during the Vietnam conflict, teaching and work with at-risk adolescents for more than thirty years, a long and enduring marriage as well as the raising of three children in rural Iowa. All these have had a lasting impact on the material that I have written.

HOUSEKEEPING
—after Lorine Niedecker

1. Turnips & Broom

>..."whether it is sweeping
> a room or pulling turnips."
> Thoreau

This world turns on turnips & broom:
      a father's winter stash,
      his cache to stave
off fear of starvation,
a mother's housekeeping crises

wearing down the stiffest of bristle tips;
      turnips in the cellar's
      nest of loose
straw & a new straw broom,
the household measured, staid.

2. Dust

> "Dust on shelves can wait until we need
> the spiritual uplift of dusting."
> Guy Davenport

With cloth, with feathers,
      with whispers
      of breath,
dust moves, shifts, dances off
to settle again, to discover itself

in place, the perfect, the ideal
        space, becalmed,
            impassive,
waiting for cloth, an idler's
finger, an awakening to usher it on.

Two Poems to Replace March

1.

How lost winter looks
with mud on her shoes. Now

the low rises in these Iowa
fields are beginning to remember
color. Mornings,

we mark the snowdrifts,
their slow fall from fences
& tree trunks
like flood waters from the levee.

Sparrows fill a bare March
elm like strangers in a lobby.
They have carried this day
in their mouths for months
faithfully.

2.

What freedom is there
in this

instinctive land? It is a nest
of arrivals. Yesterday,
our barn cat back from holiday
two farms down.

And now these three farm boys drive
yearling heifers home toward
barns on the far side of the road.

There is nothing of reason
here. We kiss & our kiss
lingers. The bull bristles,
penned.

Father-Milk

Rocking you wasn't love,
                        was
the mindless instinct in a wee
   milkman's hour
winnowing into will-o'-the-wisp
when your mother had had

enough, & you,
   whimpering,
                  were all mine.

As I rocked, I hummed
   & rehummed the *Dies Irae,*
that funereal & perverse lullaby
from the dead Latin Mass for the dead
with its fidelity of Gregorian notes,
   lock-step,
              as precise & steady
as rungs running up & down
Jacob's believable ladder.

In the pale, milk-blue hour,
I held your fine skull,
   malleable frontal & parietal bones,
firmly between my cheek & shoulder,
feeling your non-stop heart
   bounding & bounding
from the soft fontanel on top,
nursing you with the only milk I had.

Our Garden's

grackle, she complains,
darksome & drab amid the sow-
thistle, burdock, our voluminous

(but muted) dogbane.
It's the lure of the predictably
domestic, I tell her, the cruelest

pantomime as in our neighbor widow's
facial contortions
when she whispers granny-secrets

into our ears: *female
problems, private parts, passing away.*
The two of us walk out of the house

to gather up the last few bowls
of autumn raspberries,
quick & arrogant in their thorns.

Here's a lie, my love, a ruthless kiss.
We miss each other. (We hold hands.)
Huckleberries blue beneath

September suns; pullets
feather out on garden wastes & ants
in cantaloupes as cockerels

crow & crow
like rasps drawn backwards
across the ends of copper tubing.

We miss ourselves; we hold hands.
It's enough then to recite our litany
of luxuries: skittishly

silvered goats in the garden
among the remnants
of carrots & kale; three

cold nights;
crickets
in the ditch who still sing.

Reading Sunday

clouds is 19th century –
lying outside in the tall grass
with my hands pillowed behind my head
& thinking how Emily Dickinson
might have done it upstairs
in her bedroom or while walking
home after church services.
Who'ld've guessed?
The way, for instance, John Muir,
when he was only Johnny & tending
sheep for a few months in the High Sierras,
got up a journal with cloud words in it
like "bossy" and "butter-colored."
Just for fun, I've been watching
the little ones that aren't butter-
colored but angry & sitting on
the edge of the pot of sky like
mongrels exhausted with the rain.

Susan Tepper

It's always been my firm belief that the artist is called upon to do the task rather than a person making a conscious decision to become an artist. Because art, in all its myriad forms, is difficult. Not the actual making of art, which for me is always a moment of delight and abandonment, but the subsequent placement of the art, finding its appreciative audience— that is the difficult aspect. The true artists never quit because to quit would be to open a vein, to throw in the towel, on what are moments of pure creative joy. My own work is never done with any forethought. The muse or some artistic spirit lives close by and speaks to me on a pretty regular basis. I listen and move forward. Dear Petrov is a result of these unconscious writings that come from a wellspring deep within me. I never try and steer any piece to a conclusion. It is what it is.

BLUEBELLS

The child is buried near the hill where bluebells grow. It was smaller than my palm. The day hung still with yellow light. I do remember. Not quite sun and a mist hovered without moisture. I squatted knowing only in that moment. The change coming with the pain. There was no one I could tell. You were off, dear Petrov. Somewhere on the continent. I felt my body empty out. At the base of that hill. Bluebells swaying as if dancing. I thought about swallowing it. Putting it back. Letting it reconsider. Instead I did the common thing. Dug a hole with my shoe heel. Fit the child in. Covering over with dirt and grass. Pebbles. Kneeling. Watching. The place where it lay. Staying 'til the light waned. Alone. Going back to the house I boiled the tea water. Tried eating crusts spitting them into a plate. Wondering what you would say when you finally returned. If you would empty out, too. Or just continue to be a man.

Dead

What brought us to this place, dear Petrov. My complaints bounce off the deaf ears of the mountain. Always hovering. We could have chosen a meadow dotted with flowers. Or a place near the sea. Watching the waves rolling in. A cave. The mouth of the peninsula. We could have chosen the land of the dead. We live dead despite the difference in name. Dead is born when beauty goes unnoticed. Dead is when the rocks no longer hold to moss or dirt. Their shiny compliance. It pushes them down the mountainside. Tumbling. Into the path of carts and horses. Rocks to be sidestepped when out for a brief walk. Death to be sidestepped. And how tiresome a house can become. So much silence. Filth. I sing and the walls don't notice. I scream. No notice. The house fills up with so much dirt and silence. While you are away. Always away. Some place.

The Scarf

Always there is a memory of birds. I see them even when the curtains are drawn. When I'm out walking in dreams. They bring the thirst at night when there is no one. I reach for the glass on my bed table finding it empty. Despairing, I climb on my horse to tremble under his shuddering flanks. I stroke his ears and between his eyes. Letting my hand drop for his nuzzle. We walk the rooms to remember. Then out through the kitchen door into the sky. There was a time I believed in the future. All the four seasons. A watching moon. I have come to believe in nothing more than walls and mold and shadows. A roof that rattles and leaves its tiles on the ground. Mice and other scurrying things. I dress in black and carry myself with dignity. Pride. A falsehood. My scarf is black and velvet. It should bring solace. To one looking for sleep.

MIDNIGHT

We circle the room the clock on the mantel chimes midnight. My horse whinnys. Tired of walking in tight spaces I suspect. Anxious for his rest. As I am anxious for mine but not in a cold bed. Empty. A mattress that doesn't squeak when my thin frame lowers to it. Just one more I whisper into my horse's ear. It flickers like the candle on the table in a slight breeze. I brush his hairs with a fingertip. Dear Petrov you are long past the time you promised. When the lime trees turned to gold. Now vanished they are ash on the ground. Stick arms taunting me. I lower my eyes to evade them. Pull my hat veil further down my face. It will be a long time before the first buds. Before nature again tucks into the meadow. Before birds come back like schools of fish. Am I to spend each winter in this silent place. Rooms that shudder upon my entry. Only to be pitied. Is this what you see for my life dear Petrov. Or am I a victim of my own desires.

Painting

Today I saw a man painting a picture near the river. He didn't mind that I watched over his shoulder. From a short distance. The day was warm and bright. Butterflies flitted about. He said he was glad for the company. I watched him put the most glorious color on top of others. Pink on yellow on red. His river frothed like thick blue icing. Then he said the light is changed. Packed up his paints and brushes. Will you be here tomorrow I asked. He only smiled. Clenching a stick of straw in his teeth. Finally he said God willing. I watched him walk bent-backed up the river slope. Calling out 'goodbye' to him. Should God not be willing tomorrow. At least I have said my goodbye. I clenched my hands 'til his form vanished past the trees. Dear Petrov do you fear the guns and cannon fire that assault these lands. Do you whisper God willing each day and night. Or is it a matter of luck as you said after drinking too much whiskey. The very same night you talked about love.

Hat

Out in the shed my horse looks empty. I feed him new hay and potatoes from my hand. Sing him a song to cheer his poor life. His tongue feels warm and scratchy. In the town people sing and cheer themselves each night. I tether him to the trap explaining we are going into town. Telling him to remain steady while I retrieve my best hat. The one you festooned with an ostrich feather dear Petrov. Tucking it under the velvet ribbon-band. Exquisite this feather. A hat like no other. Women jealously eye this hat. Coveting it. I wear it with pride. Also for courage. Protection. Faith. It makes me joyous and that in itself would be enough. I climb in the trap and we clap down the roads into town. My horse's tail and my feather bounce in unison. I sing a few songs and we bounce more jubilantly. Pure, dear Petrov, you once said about my voice. I felt it drop down from heaven then pushing through me. That night I sang sweeter. 'Til dew drained from the flowers once the sun had risen again.

Peggy Dobreer

    These poems come from an exploration of what it means to be present in the world and to the body at the same time. As a dancer before a poet, my window into writing is often kinesthetic rather than intellectual. Internal and external landscapes can oscillate at such different rhythms at the same time that a kind of vertigo or overwhelm can set in and sort of mesmerize me. I feel like a star caught in a current of electromagnetic energy. You could say I'm exploring the kinesthesia of writing. Maybe mine are poems of dispersion?

    I do know that they have something to do with longing. And longing disperses energy. It can also make us more curious, more mobile, and more flexible. If we can really see it, write it, and share it, we find that we're never alone in it. It's comforting really, a road to intimacy with the reader.

Small Foot Falls...

"Wingtip shape affects the size and drag of its vortices."
—*Wikipedia*

along the branches
and a wingspan
folded and bound
to its own tail feather.

The hummer flew
itself into the window
Mistook its reflection
for touchstone to the body.

It felt like flying.

Sounded like a chant,
all bare bones prayer
and feather, a claw full
of travel. A parable. A coat.

A weathered shoe no
bird would ever wear,
no wing could hold up
to the trouble. And wind

did blow, like a great
light that beat against
the sky. Like something
arbitrary, or mindfull,

or heart less. A motion
without thought is
pure mother, perfect
flight, request answered.

Golden, glimmering like
a whisper, faint but sure,
on the ear of the beloved.
*Beloved, it is you. Ever
you.*

All The Frozen Little Horses

we ride away like painted
                ponies spinning off the round

breaking from prance
                to trot to canter

our glee fixed in motion
                under a pretense of chipping

paint like browns and oxblood red
                peacock and royal blue

hips locked in a frozen gallop
                bent like a crone's steel hand

grabbing the reigns at a clip
                high stepping over sacred

markers kicking them loose
                setting them free looking

aside while they roll off kilter
                acting like clowns on paint

WHEN THE LIVING BURN YOUNG

First they will lodge in
the cavity of your chest, light
weight, the life snapped out.

Hearts discover right being
in the taste of iron
on a balsam tongue.

When music begins we know
silence. Sternum is a galaxy
with spokes.

The best good-byes are prayers
for the future, or perhaps
the dying. If you will, dance.

Lean into the rungs of your DNA,
empty your saucer of torment.
You cup will be refilled. Sweetness
can be added to taste.

The Number Devil

"Robert was tired of dreaming. I always come out looking dumb, he said to himself."

-Hans Magnus Enzensberger

The first is water. The second is fire.
The third a bird in flames.

The fourth is the flame. The fifth put it out.
The sixth laid an egg like blame.

The egg is the seventh in neon disguise.
The eighth is a ratio of darkness to light.

Ninth is completion with all work showing.
Tenth is first place in a double-digit knowing.

Eleventh is a realm of jesters and paint.
On the side of a truck selling fry bread and saints.

Then, a mission, a candle, milagros that tell.
Look up, it's new, and cannot be quelled

Fifteen is old. Sixteen, as the hills.
Messages fall in a ravenous shrill

Eighteen is terrestrial. Nineteen, of the sea.
Twenty is love, the moon's eye on me.

Twenty-one is a wish that needs to be fused.
Twenty-two begs severance from what blinds and fools.

Minus a vortex, black whole on the sun,
a lie and a chalice, there's no way to run.

Twenty-five is a plan with a fearless vow.
Twenty-six is a fire. Twenty-seven. Not now.

Twenty-eight is a pity left by the road.
Twenty-nine is walking a hard way home.

And thirty is what is set free letting go.

The Dazzling

after Die Erblindende

Is it the way we are changed
whenever sipping tea? Who will be

served first diving into an unknown
cup?   There is so little warning

when change catches hold. Laughter
comes—sometimes not. Is it a crime

the way we smile or raise ourselves
to speak? How can we walk toward

birth without terror? Behavior imagines
it so. We want to sing loud into dawn.

But we walk so far behind the others,
eyes lit up like the surface of a sunlit pond

from which we soon will drink. The shadow
turns slowly, will not survive another night.

And yet with a single gesture, we see

Joseph Fasano

What do I want from a poem? Lamb's blood in a river. The moon. A rusted stirrup on an empty bed. A house in flames and all the birds flown through it. I want the body. I want a poem to hold me by the collar, to never let me forget the body. Ever. Not in this world. The tall grass by a river at dusk and the sound of an oar lifting. A horse kneeling down in its blinders on a dark shore. The thing the briar has written in its skin. That the rain will wash away by morning.

The Joy That Tends Toward Unbecoming

Say five men carry a sixth from the birches.
He is thin from his night inside the river.
Someone has pushed his wrists through his belt
so it seems he has been out gathering blue flowers.

Someone is shouting the richer gospels.
I remember a woman leaning on the window,
thinking death had loosed its bird in the house.
I remember the bird fell on the third day

and I had to line my hands with a nest of old straw.
That night they found a boy in the square
like a foal, smelling of onion grass.
Someone had let a black swan

into the barn where the boy was kept
and in the moonlight we saw dark plumage in his fists.
Say you were the wild gift, how it had quarreled
and come near. Say you had been torn.

Mahler in New York

Now when I go out, the wind pulls me
into the grave. I go out
to part the hair of a child I left behind,

and he pushes his face into my cuffs, to smell the wind.
If I carry my father with me, it is the way
a horse carries autumn in its mane.

If I remember my brother,
it is as if a buck had knelt down
in a room I was in.

I kneel, and the wind kneels down in me.
What is it to have a history, a flock
buried in the blindness of winter?

Try crawling with two violins
into the hallway of your father's hearse.
It is filled with sparrows.

Sometimes I go to the field
and the field is bare. There is the wind,
which entrusts me;

there is a woman walking with a pail of milk,
a man who tilts his bread in the sun;
there is the black heart of a mare

in the milk—or is it the wind, the way it goes?
I don't know about the wind, about the way
it goes. All I know is that sometimes

someone will pick up the black violin of his childhood
and start playing—that it sits there on his shoulder
like a thin gray falcon asleep in its blinders,

and that we carry each other this way
because it is the way we would like to be carried:
sometimes with mercy, sometimes without.

October

This is the season in which the lambs begin
to die, in which the boy in his red and blue plaid

shirt gets down on his wrists and his knees to crawl
into the moorland at night and spread a cross of pumice

on their foreheads, in which he reads to them a hymn
like a freighter burning with a cargo of ripened fruit

because in the morning he will have to kill them.
Because in the morning he will wake to find his father

standing in the hall like a horse with a lamp in its mouth
and he will have to wade into a river with only that silence

in his arms, and he will harm them. Because every year
I watch him stand at the threshold of a season and begin

to call them, to hold the ruined bodies of the dead
with only a dim chord of flame between his lips

and to touch them, to touch them
and to be with them, to touch them

and to sing with them, the way a child
touches everything, with the hand of his murderer.

The Figure

for A.L.

You sit at a window and listen to your father
crossing the dark grasses of the fields

toward you, a moon soaking through his shoes as he shuffles the wind
aside, the night in his hands like an empty bridle.

How long have we been this way, you ask him.
It must be ages, the wind answers. It must be the music of the wind

turning your fingers to glass, turning the furniture of childhood
to the colors of horses, turning them away.

Your father is still crossing the acres, a light on his tongue
like a small coin from an empire that has always been ruined.

Now the dark flocks are drifting through his shoulders
with an odor of lavender, an odor of gold. Now he has turned

as though to go, but only knelt down with the heavy oars
of October on his forearms, to begin the horrible rowing.

You sit in a chair in the room. The wind lies open
on your lap like the score of a life you did not measure.

You rise. You turn back to the room and repeat what you know:
The earth is not a home. The night is not an empty bridle

in the hands of a man crossing a field with a new moon
in his old wool. We abandon the dead. We abandon them.

Testimony

If tonight the moon should arrive like a lost guide
crossing the fields with a bitter lantern in her hand,

her irides blind, her dresses wild, lie down and listen to her
find you; lie down and listen to the body become

the promise of no other, the sleeper in the garden
in its own arms, the exile in its own autumnal house.

You have woken. But no one has woken. You are changed,
but the light of change is bitter, the changing

is the threshold into winter. Traveler, rememberer, sleeper,
tonight, as you slumber where the dead are, if the moon's hands

should discover you through fire, lie down
and listen to her hold you, the moon who has been away

so long now, the lost moon with her silver lips
and whisper, her body half in winter,

half in wool. Look at her, look at her, that drifter.
And if no one, if nothing comes to know you, if no song

comes to prove it isn't over, tell yourself, in the moon's
arms, she is no one; tell yourself, as you lose

love, it is after, that you alone are the bearer
in that changed place, you alone who have woken, and have

opened, you alone who can so love
what you are now and the vanishing that carries it away.

Hermitage

It's true there were times when it was too much
and I slipped off in the first light or its last hour
and drove up through the crooked way of the valley

and swam out to those ruins on an island.
Blackbirds were the only music in the spruces,
and the stars, as they faded out, offered themselves to me

like glasses of water ringing by the empty linens of the dead.
When Delilah watched the dark hair of her lover
tumble, she did not shatter. When Abraham

relented, he did not relent.
Still, I would tell you of the humbling and the waking.
I would tell you of the wild hours of surrender,

when the river stripped the cove's stones
from the margin and the blackbirds built
their strict songs in the high

pines, when the great nests swayed the lattice
of the branches, the moon's brute music
touching them with fire.

And you, there, stranger in the sway
of it, what would you have done
there, in the ruins, when they rose

from you, when the burning wings
ascended, when the old ghosts
shook the music from your branches and the great lie

of your one sweet life was lifted?

Margo Berdeshevsky

O voice of all night wind and rain, do you count the petals that are falling?
— *Meng Hao-Jan*

I want a poem to reach. And yes, I want it to be enough. No matter our ages or our beliefs—I will call poetry the language of the soul. That's one of my personal tenets. I don't mean that it's a choice between the sacred and the profane. I mean that it speaks a different language not bound by nations or borders. Language carved and sculpted as hard stones, built with words and images that risk and that insist on a voice that is their own. That's what I hold my breath for when I read others. What I dare to hope for from myself. Open my own cage and my nervous heart. Lead me into my own silence, first, and then—make me want to read the words aloud for others. Give the poem because it may be all I have to offer in this time that I'm alive.

The body is not safe. The skin is not safe. Not at this time. We know this. It is filled with not knowing. It wants light. And it can die. But I'm inside it. And from inside it—I'm reaching. Asking questions in many shapes and in this different language. In this small thing: poetry. I know how precarious our time and each life is. We are trying like hell to defend against our collective breaking. We are living more consciously, perhaps, but more tragically too in a time when each event insists that we are broken. But I am reaching. What occasions my work is simply being alive in my time. Our time. Wanting to find the words. Aching for—seeking words and their particular music—that might hold what we are hungry for. The soft and the very hard. A word that (might) sing—without disguise. What words might hold any wisdom I have gathered in my nakedness, and offer it up, as a poem? I'm trying, as you are—to find them.

Toni Morrison has written: "We die. That may be the meaning of life. But we do language. That may be the measure of our lives."

Blason Pour Le Corps

— Gentle, the sound of the rain —Verlaine

Clitoris, belly,
nape, taste bud,
body-beloved-bully,
how surprisingly you strut,
how unexpectedly you age—
How night rides the in and the out of you
Seine of you—doe of you
Who raped the silk in you? (Don't answer,)
blood's hummingbird
under your ribs
Body-monster, ravenous
now the hound's heartbeat
outrunning my greed
Body, inside,
thin ibis, flaming—
mirror-bitch brayer do I love you, or not?
Body my blessing   my birth day bleed.
Body my deceiver
Body my taunt
My strutter, my ogre, my mirror-bitch brayer
We're as opened as we'll ever be.
Listen. Listen.
Verlaine's—new rain.

Whisper

Why does my skin want me in her
does she know she's holding a woman in?

Not burning does she ache when the wild fires shout
Does she know how many Septembers she's given

Am I nailed inside her, cell by cell
or she, poor pale veil, sewn womb to

sky—is she mine or am I her
pet cobra whispering like rocks

in the streambed for more passion more
tenderness more friction more killing—

Do the stones and the branches want out?
Does my skin want tattoos of hard young men

or skulls or sentences or swallow-corpses
fallen—If I give her all my wars, my only

eye— will she let me sleep will she hold my
night dirges until I can remember them

When I die, skin of silk, skin of ash, skin
of my century, will she forgive me

again when the leaves are all dropped
Why have a woman in you—skin

Why not a bone mountain
Why not a better prayer than this one

If you won't answer, skin of my skin
skin of my woman-ing—

There are knives that might.

Ghazal

The handprints in ancient cave art were left by women
  —National Geographic

If the new animal voice cries for my empty bed, hear me.
If a wide red wing climbing my cotton gown stills me—hear me.

If wars in blued tongues of the night-scarved crows admit
what our mothers pretend to forget— will you hear me?

When wild horsemen, sketched beast-men, drawn by girls afraid
to tell secrets to their mothers, filled caves, did you hear me?

Secrets spread in menstrual reds on a cave's inner walls
Did the hills listen? Did you hear me?

My bed of old bloods has slept through dreams, and
revenants. One sky's thickened milk fills silence—hear me

silk-tongued as that hour ahead of our last summers—
leaves handprints—tears the riddles open—hear me.

If the smallest hands, if the last birds, if one unborn poem spills
just a little sky, we were not killed. Were born. Mother, hear me—

PULSE

Showers of snow geese.

Mirrors weren't my friends anymore, couldn't stand what they showed me, the changing flesh, thinning hair that used to reach my knees, the drowning of names in a mud-thick water mind

the shorter breaths. But the voice of my ghost was kind. He told me it would end, soon. Touch me, I begged. He didn't but the geese began to rain every day, and I hummed for the blind to come near.

Showers of snow geese. The morning sky bled them, no one else noticed or was bothered. I covered my eyes the way I always had when I passed any accident in the street, so afraid to see

anything dead. Afraid of winter branches, rotting gardens, abandoned houses. I hummed, like the purr of a crone panther on her rock on a dry mountain. Hummed, so the blind came nearer.

You want so badly to be seen you'd paint eyes on the lids of the blind, my ghost said. A baritone, sung between the notes of tumbling snow geese. He was my ghost, I heard him, I did what I was told. Always so afraid to be near in any way—to what didn't breathe. I wanted and needed to be seen alive. Praised for being. For breathing, for not killing any enemies, for being a good girl, for being

a good woman, for becoming a knowing crone. You want so badly to be seen you would paint eyes on the lids of the blind, the ghost had said. *Yes*, I mouthed. *True*.

My enemy had had a bad accident. The car had exploded on a curve and I crawled away. Soon, the geese. Soon, my ghost. Soon, the rock on a slope of a sun-warm mountain and my own low voice calling for the blind all night, until I was found holding a smallwhite dog, my trembling fingers stroking and stroking the lids of her chilled milk soft eyes.

I wanted to forgive something. Someone. I stroked the dog. I stroked my heart, until blindly it broke all the way open, and one bird fell out. It was not blind. It was dead. But it hummed.

Before and Before the Rivers

How will I sleep or write of herons?

Waking shreds to
meat torn in a wildcat's brute claw. Stilled

flesh whitening
where the stained orchid rises and withers.

When I see you, my breath tears
there between your bodies,

tatters to join your walk. If I remember
what I know of plenty and of empty,

or prowl—across scars,
how will I sleep, or write of herons?

Of leaps cut down curled red on the bright,
of road blood that moves in its breeze —be

safe this day,
friends, don't curl
and don't be killed

not this day, not after. There will be
cold wakings when your fist will haunt all

sleep. When the dun silence will leave.
I mean to see you
if ever I cannot stand with you.

This side of the new-born stream
there's no blood yet.

But let our cry
wait.
Infant, in its clairvoyant's caul.

But let our knowing—bleed.
How can we sleep, or write of the fallen?

I am without skin
today.
Your drum—deeper, and going deeper in.

There is a place where the wing tears.
And there is a day when the heron stands.

And there is a river for revolution
—the hardest love, coming in.

Bring me to the river where lives begin, where
our nakedness needs no skin, bring me to

where it begins and begins. Nameless. And coming in.
At the end of the beginnings, we dressed in long light—

a hybrid body of stars—River, where the parched
heart drank her fill, hill where the unborn
climbed.

Dusk

This is the place. No chairs.
A woman who is choosing
has sent a petal from her bloom
of conscious closing.

The woman who is choosing when
—scratches vellum. The rook stands.
The woman in the nest of
the phoenix hovers nearer
her edge like that brood of birthing

opal-throated pigeons in an empty
flower trough,
thirsty, one stair above my sill,
breaking their shells one by

one. She repeats
my words
from dusk in a jungle where
medicine leaned small against thorn trees.
Each poison growing in a forest

lives beside its antidote, we said.
I am still eager, I said.
Or the scent of hyacinth.
The woman remembering, who is

choosing when to die will
curl before leaves have blood-burned September.
Surrender by starvation,
she doesn't name her illness

only how many days.
Three more. The woman
in worn white cotton washed us in a tide pool,
brewed petals, shouted under

egrets at the edge of rain. Bon voyage to me & love
life as you live it she scribbles blue before her breath
ends a night and a day and the broken slant
dawn.

The woman who was choosing when to die.
Too young to be skeletal, skin taken wing.
Bone no longer needed. Dove.
Fire-eyed. Distant. Opal.

The root does not care
where her water comes from.
Here is another thirsty body.
Broken into morning.

Bill Yarrow

A confession: In my poems, I play fast and loose with the truth. In my poems, I lie freely without contrition. Better to sacrifice the truth to save the poem than to adhere strictly to the actual and sew "true facts" (who really cares?) into a corpse. Thus, the details in these poems are mostly false.

I don't always write story poems, but when I do these are the types of stories I tell.

I. Stories Based on Facts:

1. "The Hotel Where Esenin Hanged Himself" tells of the story of two Soviet poets, Sergei Alexandrovich Esenin (1895 –1925) and Vladimir Vladimirovich Mayakovsky (1893 –1930), who, while being poetic rivals, were also mirror images of each other.

2. "Maurice Utrillo" imagines the French painter with his mother Susanne Valadon. Beyond those two facts, the poem is wholly imagined.

3. "Noir vs Noir" conflates two stories—the story of the last hours of John Dillinger and the 1946 film *The Blue Dahlia*. Dillinger was shot to death on July 22, 1934 by FBI agents as he exited the Biograph Theater in Chicago where he and Polly Hamilton had been watching *Manhattan Melodrama*. The references in the poem to skin grafts and plastic surgery are real. In *The Blue Dahlia*, a famous noir written by Raymond Chandler and directed by George Marshall, Buzz Wanchek (Bendix) does hold the sides of his head and bellow, "Turn off that monkey music!"

II. Falsehoods: Autobiographical, Biographical, and Other

1. "What the Hell Am I Doing?": I have a daughter and she is a therapist, but she is not the therapist in this poem. Neither has the dialogue recounted ever occurred. The twenty poems described are poems I have published. The inspiration for this poem is Yeats's "The Circus Animals' Desertion."

2. "We Don't Need No Education": I teach and I have students, but there the resemblances between the events depicted in this poem and my personal and professional life end.

3. "The Man Whose Wife Lived in His Neck": A fantasy inspired by an interpolated tale in David Foster Wallace's *The Broom of the System*.

The Hotel Where Esenin Hanged Himself

I walk by the hotel where Esenin hanged himself.
They remodeled it so foreigners wouldn't have access
to his despair. He first tried slashing his wrists.
That didn't work. Blood flew everywhere: counters,
chairs, sheets. He sopped it up with his hands,
wrote eight red lines on the walls. Then he smashed
the mirrors. This was in 1925. He was thirty years old.

Dawn in St. Petersburg looks a lot like midnight.

It's four years later. Mayakovsky has been writing
poems to counter Esenin, "to make Esenin's end
uninteresting." Of course, he fails. Then he looks
square at the world and decides it's not for him either;
leaves a note: "Against the everyday has crashed
of love my boat," pulls a pistol and shoots himself.
The bullet ricochets off the ceiling and breaks his heart.

When writers look in mirrors, they stare at ghosts.

We Don't Need No Education

You were sitting with your vexed complexion,
your dour shoulders, your hoarse aloneness
in the front row of my English for Unwed Mothers
class, and I hadn't yet read your essay on "Miscarriages
of Injustice," nor had you read Montaigne's "That Men
Are Justly Punished for Being Obstinate in the Defense
of a Fort That Is Not in Reason To Be Defended," and it
wasn't yet Thursday 2004 when we would be sitting
on the curb in front of The Sikh Community Café
where you were telling me, "The body is a lost temple
of bliss and blister," and the smile on my face was palpably
inapt, and I blurted out, "There's an ill energy that emanates
from your precise heart that I find attractive," to which
you replied, editing me with a surgeon's cruel disinterest,
"You mean it's an attractive ill energy," and I said, "Yes,
that's what I mean," though that wasn't at all what I meant
and the sun was pursuing the moon in an ineffable dance
of unlikelihood and redress, and you were wearing
your father's shoes though I remember thinking what
large feet you had, learning later that that was unfair
and untrue, learning later that your heart, like all hearts,
was fuzzy, not precise, that your candor was a sham,
that you were neither a mother nor unmarried, that my
interest in you was not interest at all but usury, that I was
a man not in full but in fullishness, a false Montaigne,
whose chin beard, though elegant, was the merest bravado.

Maurice Utrillo

At him always, pestering him with unanswerable questions, why does he paint this, why doesn't he paint that, he doesn't know, he just paints, things that strike him, the things he sees, a dim shadow on a monument, twisted sunlight on an awning, the blue hieroglyphics of decay, a cat in the wine, the white endless façade of homes, the pink and grey of skies in love with loneliness. She watches as he stirs. Oblivious of everything, he rises, washes out his eyes, pours water through a spoon of sugar into his glass and begins to sip his pale-green drink. Absinthe makes the heart grow fonder. His canvas parts its lips and puckers. He grabs his Muse by the waist and pulls her toward him, presses his middle against her middle, his chest against her breasts, digs his fingers into her curls, pulls at the elastic of her blouse, her shoulders, suddenly, shockingly bare, her lower throat open to his open mouth, she's all a mess, dishabille, his hurried fingers take up the brush, a splash of paint, a daub of color, sips of silver, hatch of black, a wipe of white, lush squares of pastel tints, the second-story windows begin to form, enfeebled trees sprout up, the horizon is firmly planted behind the alley, around the corner, just beneath the burgeoning sky. What does this mean? What does what mean? Where are the people? They have not yet been born. Overhead, mawkish gulls begin to weep daylight into the marsh. The gutters blush as men in bloody aprons take their business to their walls. Priests in red robes bend their tonsures toward eternity, or so it seems to him, supine, head wedged against the bookcase, mouth agape, dreaming of dangers, his feet perpendicular to the floor.

The Man Whose Wife Lived in His Neck

This is the story of the man whose wife lived in his neck. Every morning, he would turn to her and say, "Hello, Sweetheart. How was your night?" and she would answer, *Brilliant! What else?* by which she meant she didn't sleep a wink but rather thought unceasingly through the long darkness and solved each of the burdens he would face during his day. In that way, he was protected from harm, and affection toward her swelled in his heart. What a comfort to have his wife not even a muscle away from his attention. Their marriage thrived, but unlike other successful ventures in the world, this one was never in danger of collapse. There would be no shift in interest or intent. Symbiotic happiness was the key, for he continually manipulated and massaged her, touching her where she ached to be touched, kneading her where she needed to be kneaded. Then one day, she informed him that she wanted to move. "Where?" he asked. *To the other side, she answered.* "It won't be the same over there," he cautioned, and it wasn't. From over there, he neither looked nor sounded the same. Something in him had altered and not for the better. She began, though the descent was gradual, to sleep lower and lower. She rested in his shoulder now where he was meatier and where it was harder for him to hear her breathing. Her protection thinned to a threadbare covering, more irritant than asset. He wanted to dig into her, but she was impossible to reach, so deep had she sunk into him. Would it only be a matter of time until she completely dissolved and joined the others in his blood? Who would he look to when, in pain, he twisted and itched? Suddenly, he felt something behind him. She had turned the corner and lodged just below the hair on the back of his head. That felt just perfect. That felt just right. That just felt fine. "Hello, Sweetheart," he said. "How was your night?" *My night? How was my night? Dazzling! Dazzling!*

Noir vs. Noir

You're sitting in a darkened theatre with Gothic ceilings and one exit watching the latest Alan Ladd film with William Bendix and Veronica Lake. Next to you eating popcorn is a woman from Romania named Anna. She is smiling but at all the wrong scenes. You put your arm around her and smile yourself. Yesterday's plastic surgery has been a complete success. The fingertip skin grafts feel the best they ever have. Bendix, a narrative madness in his eyes, is suffering from a war wound. He holds both sides of his head and bellows, "Turn off that monkey music!" The movie's good, but you don't like being in the dark. You motion to Anna to go, a shade brutally perhaps, and drag her down the aisle. In the lobby, empty but for the concessionaire, she says wait, she has to relieve herself. "Hurry it up," you mutter and pass the time staring at your face in the mirrored walls. It's not your face and that suits you just fine. "Where is she?" you wonder. At that moment she returns. "What took you?" you rasp and begin walking. "Hey, wait," she calls, running up to your side. She's pressed up against you as you push open the glass door and walk out. Something smells funny in the night. It's your future, but no one will be able to convince you of that.

What the Hell am I Doing?

> "Can you make no use of nothing, nuncle?"
> —King Lear, Act I, scene iv

My daughter is a therapist. She's started reading my
poems. She's noticed something curious: in each of them,
the same thing happens: nothing. In one, she tells me,
after a bad car accident, a woman just stares at her hands.
In another, a man travels three thousand miles looking
for a key; then when he finds it, he refuses to use it.
In another, a man sits in a plush chair happily watching
a blank screen. There's another where a boy boards a bus
and just stares out the window. A man bleeding into his
boots stands still on a foothill. An atheist gets stung by a bee
and silently watches his hand swell up. A son returns home
to a mad father. A college boy watches his grandmother die.
A despairing writer sees acorns fall from a tree. A man
with a blonde moustache loiters by rusty monkey bars.
A man (he's just learned that his mother has died in a fire)
smokes a cigarette in the cold. A man strolls past a hotel
famous because a suicide happened there. Of course, she
notices, some things do happen. Someone is slapped,
someone fakes incontinence, someone takes a cruise,
someone drinks poison on a bet. After a beautiful dream,
someone wakes up crying, someone gambles at a casino,
someone swims in the ocean. Two people almost drown.
These are alternative nothings, she tells me. "Is that a
technical term?" I ask, wondering what the criterion is
not to be nothing. "You want me to write about something?
Is that it?" *No, not necessarily. But I don't like to see you
writing about nothing.* "Why? Johnson said you need something
to fill up the vacuity of life." *And you choose nothing with which
to fill life's empty bucket?* "Maybe nothing just picked me."
I find you curious, Dad. "That's not anything either, Sweetie."

Susan Cohen

These poems are all included in *A Different Wakeful Animal*, a collection that explores what perishes and what endures. Looking at them together here, I realize how often that exploration leads me, by varying paths, to fire and light. You make these sorts of discoveries when you let a poem take off on its own until it begins to surprise you.

The thrill of words called me back to poetry after a career as a journalist. From journalism, I bring my belief in precision and clarity and my habits of revision. But poetry allows me to stretch the language and to express what cannot be described in prose, to follow my ear and the inexplicable logic of imagery rather than my purely analytic brain. In early drafts, I let a poem startle me and hurtle me along. I hope to discover connections, not forge towards a preconceived destination. After that, I revise, sometimes for weeks, more often for months, hoping the poem in its polished version will be meaningful to others as well as myself.

When I say meaningful, I'm thinking of the Russian poet Osip Mandelstam who wrote that meaning is not the same in poetry as in prose, and that when a poem can be paraphrased, "the sheets have not been rumpled, poetry has not spent the night." Poetry is a different way to see and hear the world, but I also want to share what I've seen and heard with other people. Some of my poems lean more on narrative, some are more lyrical, but typically I ground them in time and place while also encouraging language to take flights. I hope readers will find both music and meaning here—even joy—and perhaps evidence that poetry has visited and spent the night.

The Golden Hills of California

This light began in lamentation,
but I don't want to think
about the unmaking, the burning
hopes and homes a hundred miles
from here. This light is strangely
sewn with honey as if thimbled
from the flight of bees. It drifts down
through maples and the cedar,
burnishes our scarred floorboards
to yellow oak this morning,
our walls to butter. In the fabled state
we live in, somewhere always is on fire—
dry grasses torching, shingles searing,
latches melting, miles of forest
reduced to the single syllable of ash—
while elsewhere that combustion blends
light and gold we can savor like wine,
which also begins with crushing.

Tensed in Black and White

A spiraling rind, a swan midstream,
a porcelain pot feverish with tea—
and how I love the way a camera maps
in black and white a body's mounds,
nipples, aureoles, the lens's lasting
lust for light and shadow.

In one book, a photographer searched
a face for the other face inside, caught
and shot his own reflection in an eye,
while, lurking above a cigarette, a plume
defies the breeze that blew or blows
and keeps billowing a curtain.

No single tense for the lingering trope
of smoke after the fire is extinguished.
For the vigil kept by a silhouette
snapped on a 1930's Paris sidewalk.
For film found in a forgotten camera
where, fifty years ago, my cousin posed

all this time in tie and wide lapels holds still.

Describe a Holy Building

Not the looming, gloomy church I visited in Rome, with its coin slot
and sign offering *illumination*, its grimy Caravaggio in the corner
lit on a timer like a peep show.

Ah, Caravaggio— he who stranded the saint in darkness and exalted
the rump of the ass—value, a measure of color's lightness or shade:
Where the light falls I will paint it.

As I believe in liturgies of light: Sun beneficent under a steeple of spruce,
night vault pearly with moon, silver pews of waves, prophecy brilliant
in the mouths of fish.

Not the temple casting its monumental shadow, not the booming voice
scolding from the bush. But the bush—its edifice of branches flaming
into flower—that holy burning.

We Descend

The guide lifts his lantern:
A mare, her mane and
sloping muzzle thick black.

Her straight spine
holds against the sway
of a belly round with foal.

She is a pinto.
Someone painted her
with charcoal, ochre, fat

and spit. Someone breathing
this fungal air and lit by fire
in the Stone Age drew

a wakeful fish who swims
across the limestone
when the lantern swings.

We have invented nothing,
Picasso cried, emerging
from a cave like this.

They left palm prints,
their fingers splayed
as if waiting to be counted.

We resist the urge
to place our astonished
hands on theirs.

Rustin Larson

There seems to be two different kinds of poems represented in this portfolio. One kind comes from observation and the allowing of events to unfold in real time ("Searching the Library for Vandalism," "Sunday at the End of July"), as if the poet (I) were a crayfish waiting and watching in his little sandy pool in a mountain stream. I am a librarian, and notebooks have been filled as I waited and watched and recollected during my evening shift, as I observed university students and their partners and babies (like "Vincento") come and go and do what they do.

Another kind of poem is the poem of dream language and dream images ("Your Mind on Dreams," "Rain"). These other poems take longer to write. They sometimes evolve over the course of several years, maybe five to seven, and they as language are observed like a chessboard where one move, one change of a word, alters the entire game. Sometimes, oftentimes, these poems steer toward some sort of form though they don't always purely arrive there—sonnets, sestinas—but the template of the forms allow such dreams to evolve, with any luck, in a highly charged language.

I do a lot of dismantling and rebuilding and a lot of daydreaming. My best hope is that each poem serves as a kind of pub where I can hoist a metaphorical Guinness with you, smoke half a pack of metaphorical cigarettes, squint my ghostly smile, and tell you my meditations and dreams.

Dallas

A small Chinese boy pushes his suitcase through the terminal.
In a grotto, in a garden, a perfectly black butterfly hovers
over a climbing rose bush. I walk with Caroline.
Petals flat like palms held out, waiting for the touch of rain.
The noise of hundreds of people on cell phones.
They shout at each other. I take Caroline's photograph.
Announcements for boarding the aircraft. The black butterfly
touches the head of a stone saint. Everyone seems to be
in a state of suppressed delirium. There are patterns in the wind.
Businessmen hover inches from the ground like whirling blades.
There is nothing I can do. The boy pushes his suitcase.
I hear the cry of wet stone steps, touch the tip of my finger with my tongue.

SEARCHING THE LIBRARY FOR VANDALISM

One Chinese student, in gray-green camo hoodie,
Sleeps on the garish orange couch in the lounge.
Two black books lie rakishly on the floor below
A shelf full of lamp-yellow Toulouse-Lautrec.
Some damaged blue cassette tapes about escaping
Debt lie jumbled on the white Masonite give-away.
The spiny paper fish are spawning again
In the green recycle bins. An Australian patiently
Feeds a roll of Canadian nickels to the photocopier
Before it goes into a coma. Meanwhile, Herman Hesse
And Rilke wait nervously on the German literature
Shelf, as if for a tram that never quite comes,
And night is starting to get cold and starry.

Sunday at the End of July

The neighbor gets his mini-bike out
And buzzes around the yard like a wasp.
I sit breathing. Perhaps Caroline and I
Will walk to Chautauqua to see what's growing.
My drumsticks are on the floor.
I bang on things: books,
Shelves, tables, my chest.
Am I alive or not?
Caroline and I walk through the tunnel
Of trees in Chautauqua. Fireflies drift
Toward us, blinking. The trees shower us
With a fine mist. One or two birds
Are still singing. At the end of the tunnel,
A streetlamp electrifies an oak tree:
Sleepless, phosphorescent, absinthe green.

Rain

Like tumbling stones; the icy silence; rake,
Chinese fan, cascade of bramble, flatbeds of lumber
rumble in the flashing shower, vines of endless roads,
the stations of the cross, percussionist
of the forest, wild heart. This afternoon, rain, like it won't end.
Thin braid of smoke from the cottage. I ponder your quiet dignity,
polished window looking down at me,
a valentine homesick for clouds. Geodes, agate,
this afternoon in Paradise, rain. You recall
the turquoise cemented under the fires of creation.
The graves whisper wild grasses, rain-thirsty.
Violent flowers, one more season,
another life we've lived, boxcar after boxcar. In the big lake
raindrops drown without memories,
without lingering colors, without names.

Vincento Looks Unhappy

Vincento looks unhappy in his radioactive suit; not
Even the dragon of rainbow hexagons can brighten
His day, even by offering a hexagon of gelatinous
Fruit-flavored goop. Vincento still frowns. He
Frowns even though in the clouds above him frolic
Fluffy maidens in lace and twins in love with their
Discovery of a wheel of gorgonzola. Not even the
Hockey-playing knight or the smiling rubber daisy
Or the dinosaur with the three-pack habit can make
Him smile. Vincento, the flies that circle you are
Made of diamonds.

Your Mind on Dreams

The moon withers, and when it's dark you read
In bed. There's too much spilling o'er your sides.
You read down to the creek, dragging
Your four-poster. It will not be so long:

The ceiling of moonlight, the fox-eyed
Dreams mewing in umber. Summer is rotund.
The siren spreads its flash of red. The creeks
Of India ink run, maidens of mist

And sleep, your list of laws and mirror. Night
Trickles forward. You won't recognize the sun
When you wake, or how the trees have become
A different room, or how their scent is on you

Something like a stain, a handprint, a ghost,
A goddess of rivers, a song broken.

Publication Credits

Margo Berdeshevsky

"Blason Pour Les Corps," originally published in *Prairie Schooner*

"Pulse," originally published in *Plume*

"Dusk," originally published in *The Academy of American Poets Poem-For-a-Day* [selected by the chancellors]

Susan Cohen

"The Golden Hills of California" originally appeared in *Redactions: Poetry & Poetics, Vol. 19.*

"We Descend" originally appeared in *[Ex]tinguished and [Ex]tinct; An Anthology of Things That No Longer [Ex]ist* (Twelve Winters Press; 2014)

Peggy Dobreer

"All The Frozen Little Horses" was published under an earlier title in *The Poetry Circus Anthology*, Yak Press, September 19, 2015, ISBN # 978-0-9837904-4-0

"The Dazzling" in *Pirene's Fountain* Volume 8, Issue 16

Joseph Fasano

"The Joy That Tends Toward Unbecoming" from *Fugue for Other Hands* (Cider Press, 2013)

"Mahler in New York" from *Fugue for Other Hands* (Cider Press, 2013)

"October" from *Fugue for Other Hands* (Cider Press, 2013)

"The Figure" from *Inheritance* (Cider Press, 2014)

"Testimony," *The Academy of American Poets poem-a-day*, 2014

"Hermitage," *The Academy of American Poets poem-a-day*, 2015

Gail Goepfert

"Drinking It In" published in Room Magazine 2014 as "Plenitude"

"Get Up Said the World" published in Blue Lyra Review as "Revivify"

"In the Glass of My Eye" published in Blue Heron Review as "Vitreous"

Rustin Larson

"Dallas" and "Rain" in Lyrical Iowa

"Vincento Looks Unhappy" in Poets & Artists

Nicole Rollender

"Psalm to Be Read as My Daughter Looks at Her Ribs," Rogue Agent, April 2015

"The Return," Word Riot, May 2015

"Bone of My Bone," The Journal, Spring 2015

"How to Talk to Your Dead Mother," Harpur Palate, Spring 2015

"This Is How to Feed Your Young," ELJ Publications' Black Orchid Designs: A Broadside Series

"Reading Vallejo, On Having No Desires," MiPOesias, December 2014

Terry Savoie

"Housekeeping," North American Review

"Two Poems to Replace March," Black Warrior Review

"Father-Milk," Poetry (Chicago)

"Our Garden's," Ascent

"Reading Sunday," The Amicus Journal (currently OnEarth)

Bill Yarrow

"Maurice Utrillo" was first published in Pirene's Fountain (Volume 7, issue 16).

"The Hotel Where Esenin Hanged Himself" was first published in Connotation Press and appears in Pointed Sentences (BlazeVOX 2012).

"We Don't Need No Education" was first published in Blue Fifth Review and appears in Incompetent Translations and Inept Haiku (Červená Barva Press 2013).

"What the Hell Am I Doing?" was published in Gargoyle #61 and appears in Incompetent Translations and Inept Haiku (Červená Barva Press 2013) and Blasphemer (Lit Fest Press 2015).

Contributor Notes

Margo Berdeshevsky, born in New York city, often writes in Paris. Her newest poetry manuscript was a finalist for the National Poetry Series, 2015. Her published poetry collections are *Between Soul & Stone*, and *But a Passage in Wilderness* (Sheep Meadow Press). Her book of illustrated stories, *Beautiful Soon Enough* (University of Alabama Press), received Fiction Collective Two's Innovative Fiction Award. Other honors include the Robert H. Winner Award from the Poetry Society of America, the *& Now Anthology of the Best of Innovative Writing*, numerous Pushcart prize nominations for works in *Poetry International*, *New Letters*, *Kenyon Review*, *The Collagist*, *Tupelo Quarterly*, *Gulf Coast*, *Pleiades*, *Prairie Schooner*, among others. In Europe her work has been seen in *The Poetry Review* (UK) *The Wolf*, *Europe*, *Siècle 21*, & *Confluences Poétiques*. A multi genre novel, *Vagrant*, is patiently at the gate. Her "Letters from Paris" may be seen in Poetry International here: http://pionline.wordpress.com/category/letters-from-paris/ She may be found reading from her books in London, Paris, New York City, or somewhere new—in the world. For more information, kindly see: http://margoberdeshevsky.blogspot.com/

Susan Cohen lives in Berkeley where she was a newspaper reporter, contributing writer to the *Washington Post Magazine*, and professor at the University of California Graduate School of Journalism before spending a year on a Knight Fellowship at Stanford University, dividing her time between studying poetry and bioethics. Since then, she's co-authored *Normal at Any Cost*, which won awards from the Fund for Investigative Journalism and the National Association of Science Writers; and published two chapbooks and a full-length volume of poetry, *Throat Singing* (WordTech; 2012). In 2013, she earned an MFA from Pacific University. Her poems have won honors and appeared in dozens of publications, including *Greensboro Review*, *Los Angeles Review*, *Poet Lore*, *River Styx*, *Southern Humanities Review*, *Southern Poetry Review*, *Verse Daily*, and the *Bloomsbury Anthology of Contemporary Jewish American Poetry*. Her second full-length collection, *A Different Wakeful Animal*—finalist for the Philip Levine Prize, the Richard Snyder Award, and the May Swenson Award among others—won the 2015 David Martinson-Meadowhawk Prize from Red Dragonfly Press, which will publish it in 2016.

Peggy Dobreer came to poetry late and inevitably through dance and experimental theatre. She was nominated for a pushcart in 2014. Two years prior, Moon Tide Press released her first book, *In The Lake of Your Bones*. Peggy is a long time educator, offering a physically mindful poetry experience in her E=Mc2Bodied Poetry Workshops. Her most recent anthology inclusions are *Pirene's Fountain*, and *Like A Girl, Perspectives On Feminine Identity*, Lucid Moose Lit. Peggy was a Program Director at AROHO2015 Retreat for Women Writers at Ghost Ranch in New Mexico. Peggy's poetry has been published in *The Bicycle Review, Mas Tequilla Review, The Nervous Breakdown, The San Pedro River Review, WordWright's Magazine, Malpais Review*, and *LA Yoga Magazine* among others. She has been interviewed for *Poetiscape, The Nervous Breakdown, The Poet's Café* on KPFK, and the *L.A. Poetry Examiner*. She is proud to be included in Matthew Mars' Haiku Remix Project. Peggy hosts The RwIrGiHtTe Read at Stories Books. She currently teaches for Red Hen Press in their Writing in the Schools Program. For contact information please visit her at www.peggydobreer.com.

Joseph Fasano is the author of three books of poetry: *Vincent* (Cider Press, 2015); *Inheritance* (2014), and *Fugue for Other Hands* (2013), which won the Cider Press Review Book Award and was nominated for the Poets' Prize, awarded annually for the "best book of verse by an American poet." His poems have appeared in *The Yale Review, The Times Literary Supplement, The Southern Review, Boston Review, Tin House, FIELD*, and the anthology *Poem-a-Day: 365 Poems of Any Occasion* (Abrams, 2015). A winner of the *RATTLE* Poetry Prize, he has been featured in the Academy of American Poets' poem-a-day program, Verse Daily, and the PEN Poetry Series. He teaches at Columbia University and Manattanville College.

Gail Goepfert is a poet, amateur photographer, and teacher. Currently, she is an associate editor of *RHINO Poetry*. Her first chapbook, *A Mind on Pain*, was released by Finishing Line Press in 2015. Her recent publications include *Ardor, After Hours, Caesura, Crab Orchard Review, Florida English, Jet Fuel Review, Examined Life Journal, Pirene's Fountain, Vine Leaves Literary Journal,* and *Room Magazine*. Her teaching of poetry in the classroom grew into an eight-year extracurricular group called Dreamcatchers, eighth graders interested in writing and publishing poetry. A Pushcart Prize has come her way twice. Her photographs appear in print or online at the Chicago Botanic Garden, *Olentangy Review, 3Elements Review, After Hours Press,* and *Rattle*. In photography and writing, nature is her teacher.

Rustin Larson's poetry has appeared in *The New Yorker, The Iowa Review, North American Review, Poetry East,* and *The American Entomologist Poet's Guide to the Orders of Insects*. He is the author of *The Wine–Dark House* (Blue Light Press, 2009), *Crazy Star* (selected for the Loess Hills Book's Poetry Series in 2005), *Bum Cantos, Winter Jazz, & The Collected Discography of Morning*, winner of the 2013 Blue Light Book Award (Blue Light Press, San Francisco), and *The Philosopher Savant* (Glass Lyre Press, 2015).

Nicole Rollender's work has appeared in *The Adroit Journal, Alaska Quarterly Review, Best New Poets, The Journal, THRUSH Poetry Journal, West Branch, Word Riot* and others. Her first full-length collection, *Louder Than Everything You Love*, was published by ELJ Publications in 2015. She's the author of the poetry chapbooks Arrangement of *Desire* (Pudding House Publications, 2007), *Absence of Stars* (dancing girl press & studio, 2015), *Bone of My Bone*, a winner in Blood Pudding Press's 2015 Chapbook Contest, and *Ghost Tongue* (Porkbelly Press, 2016). She has received poetry prizes from *CALYX Journal, Ruminate Magazine* and *Princemere Journal*.

Over the past thirty-five years, **Terry Savoie** has had more than three hundred poems published in literary journals, small press publications and anthologies including *Poetry* (Chicago), *Ploughshares, The Iowa Review, Prairie Schooner, APR* and *Great River Review*. He is a retired teacher now living just outside Iowa City with Donna, his spouse of more than forty-five years.

Susan Tepper's poetry, fiction, interviews and essays have been published by the hundreds worldwide. She is the author of five published books of fiction and a chapbook of poetry. Awards include 7th Place Winner in the Zoetrope Contest for the Novel (2006), and Second Place Winner in storySouth Million Writers Award (2014). Tepper has received nine Pushcart Nominations and a Pulitzer Nomination for her epistolary novel *What May Have Been'* (Cervena Barva Press, 2010). Her column "Let's Talk," about all things writerly, runs monthly at *Black Heart Magazine,* and Tepper is the founder and host of FIZZ a reading series at KGB Bar, NYC these past eight years. Susan's work here also appears in her new book of linked pieces titled *dear Petrov* published by Pure Slush Books, Australia. www.susantepper.com

Bill Yarrow, Professor of English at Joliet Junior College and six-time Pushcart Prize and Best of the Net nominee, is the author of *Blasphemer, Pointed Sentences,* and four chapbooks. His poems have appeared in many print and online magazines including *Pirene's Fountain, Poetry International, RHINO, Contrary, Altered Scale, DIAGRAM, FRiGG, THRUSH Poetry, Gargoyle, Iodine Poetry Journal,* and *PANK*. He is featured in Derek Alger's *Beginnings: How 14 Poets Got Their Start* and Michele MacDannold's *This is Poetry: Volume II: The Midwest Poets* and is an editor at *Blue Fifth Review*.

Glass Lyre Press

exceptional works to replenish the spirit

Glass Lyre Press is an independent literary publisher interested in technically accomplished, stylistically distinct, and original work. Glass Lyre seeks diverse writers that possess a dynamic aesthetic and an ability to emotionally and intellectually engage a wide audience of readers.

Glass Lyre's vision is to connect the world through language and art. We hope to expand the scope of poetry and short fiction for the general reader through exceptionally well-written books, which evoke emotion, provide insight, and resonate with the human spirit.

Poetry Collections
Poetry Chapbooks
Select Short & Flash Fiction
Anthologies

www.GlassLyrePress.com

www.ingramcontent.com/pod-product-compliance
Lightning Source LLC
Chambersburg PA
CBHW021156080526
44588CB00008B/363